MAGNETS

By

Steffi Cavell-Clarke

©2017
Book Life
King's Lynn
Norfolk PE30 4LS

ISBN: 978-1-78637-105-8

All rights reserved
Printed in Malaysia

Written by:
Steffi Cavell-Clarke

Edited by:
Grace Jones

Designed by:
Danielle Jones

A catalogue record for this book
is available from the British Library

PHOTO CREDITS

Abbreviations: l-left, r-right, b-bottom,
t-top, c-centre, m-middle.

Front cover – Alan Bailey. 2 – Sergey Novikov. 4 – Brian A Jackson. 5– Tom
Wang. 6 – James Steidl. 7 – Asier Romero. 8tl – nanantachoke 8tr – donikz
8bl – design56 8br –. Antonsov85. 9 – nanantachoke. 10/11 – Bborriss.67.
12 – Joachim Wendler. 13 – design56. 14 – MilanB. 15 – Lemau Studio.
16 – MilanB. 17 – revers. 18 – takasu. 19t – revers 19b – DenisNata.
20 – Szekeres Szabolcs. 21 – Tatyana Vyc. 22l – Fedorov Oleksiy 22m – Picsfive.
22r – Africa Studio 22b– Fat Jackey. 23 – Scott Rothstein.
Images are courtesy of Shutterstock.com.
With thanks to Getty Images, Thinkstock Photo and iStockphoto.

CONTENTS

Words that look like this can be found in the glossary on page 24.

What is SCIENCE?

What can magnets do?

What does a magnet look like?

What does "magnetic" mean?

Science can answer many difficult questions we may have and help us to understand the world around us.

What is a
MAGNET?

A magnet is a piece of **metal** which **attracts**
or **repels** other metals, such as iron and steel.

A magnet makes a force. A force can make things move. You cannot see a force but you can see and feel its **effects**.

7

What Does a  Look Like?

A magnet is made out of metal and can come in many different shapes and sizes.

8

You will usually see them in a bar shape or a horseshoe shape.

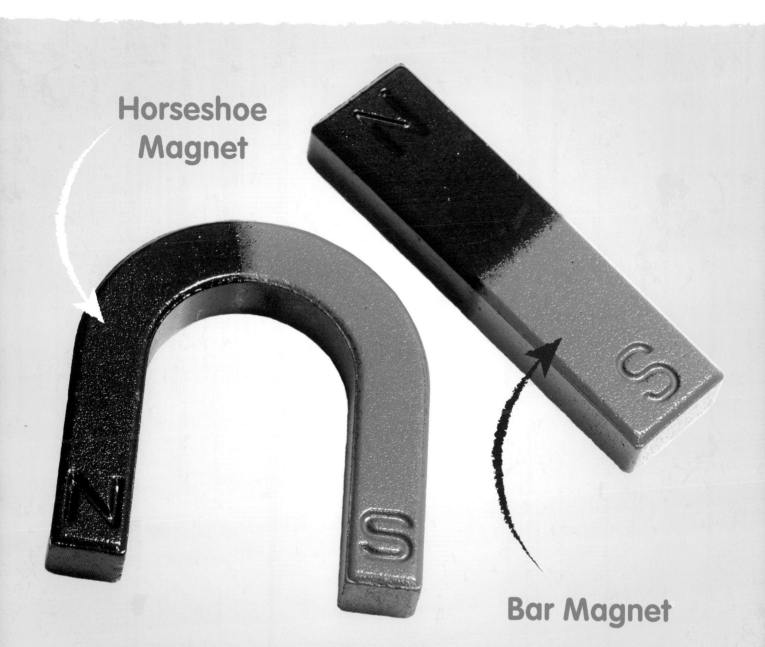

Horseshoe Magnet

Bar Magnet

What are MAGNETIC POLES?

South Pole

Every magnet has two parts.
These are called magnetic poles.

North Pole

One side of the magnet is called the north pole and the other side is called the south pole.

What is
ATTRACTION?

Attraction happens when
two **objects** are pulled together.

A magnet's north pole attracts the south pole of another magnet.

How Do MAGNETS Repel?

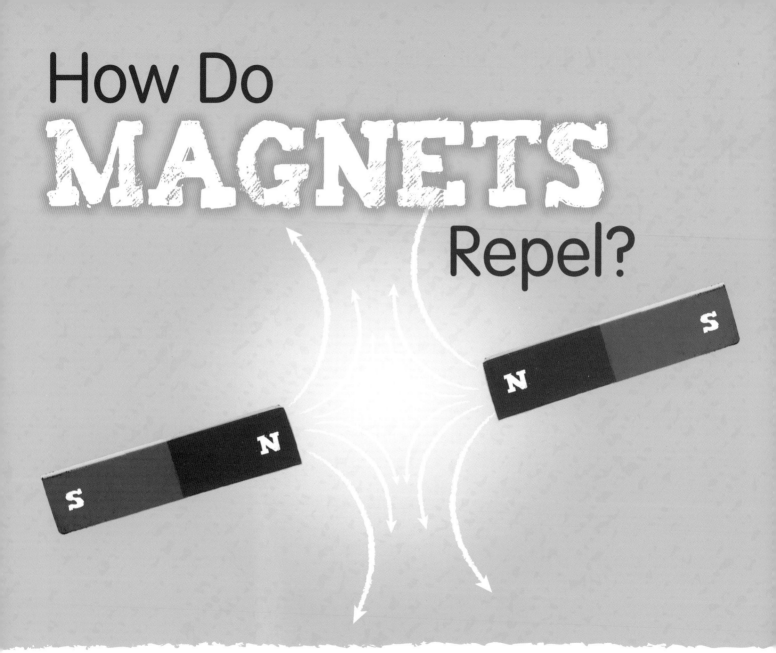

The north pole of a magnet will repel the north pole of another magnet. This is the same when the south poles of two different magnets meet.

This means that the two magnets will push away from each other.

What is MAGNETIC?

When something is attracted to a magnet it is magnetic.

Iron and steel are types of metal which are magnetic. This means that any object made with iron or steel will be attracted to a magnet.

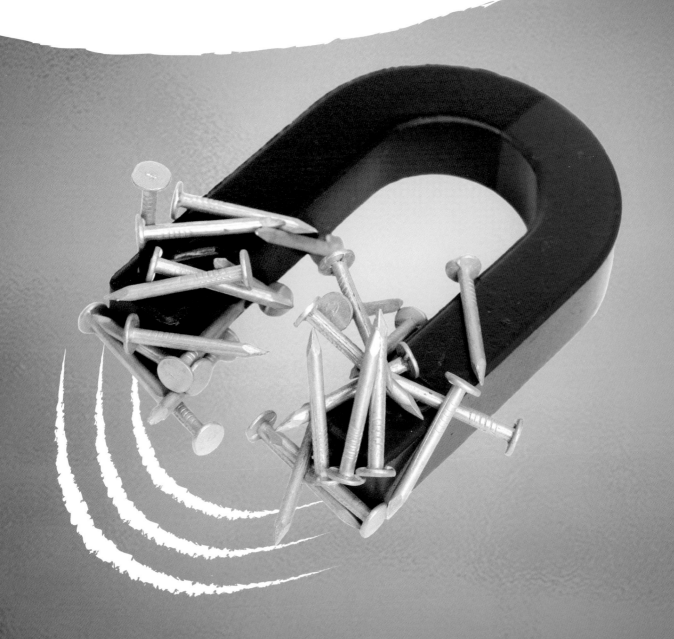

A magnet can be used to test whether something is magnetic or not. A magnet will attract a paperclip because the paperclip is made of metal and is magnetic.

A magnet will not attract a wooden pencil.

A magnet will not attract wood, because wood is not a magnetic material.

Using MAGNETS

Magnets are used for many things, like keeping fridge doors shut.

There are magnets inside the fridge door which pull the door towards the door frame to keep it shut.

Let's EXPERIMENT!

Do you know which objects are magnetic? Let's find out!

YOU WILL NEED:
A magnet
Paper
Spoon
Paperclip
Five pence piece
Leaf

STEP 1
Place all of your objects in front of you.

STEP 2
Place your magnet on each one and slowly lift it up.

22

RESULTS:

Were any of the objects attracted to the magnet? This experiment will show you that some materials such as paper are not magnetic. However, you will also see how magnets attract some materials made from metal.

GLOSSARY

attracts pulls together
effects the results of something
metal a natural material used to make things
objects things that can be seen and touched
repels pushes away